PIANO
VOCAL
GUITAR

REBECCA ST. JAMES PRAY

ISBN 0-634-00243-0

HAL•LEONARD®
CORPORATION
7777 W. BLUEMOUND RD. P.O. BOX 13819 MILWAUKEE, WI 53213

Pray

Words and Music by REBECCA ST. JAMES,
MICHAEL QUINIAN and TEDD TJORNHOM

Slowly, Very Freely

Moderately Fast

Je - sus, I am brok - en now. __ Be - fore __

* Vocal line written one octave higher than sung

Original key: Db major. This edition has been transposed down one half-step to be more playable.

-sus, I am brok - en now ___ be - fore ___ You.

OK

Words and Music by REBECCA BOUCHER,
BEVERLY BOUCHER and ANDREW THOMSON

Give Myself Away

Words and Music by PETER MORGAN,
REBECCA ST. JAMES and PAUL A. CLAESGNES

Original key: G♯ minor. This edition has been transposed up one half-step to be more playable.

give my-self a-way ___ to You to - day. ___

Hold Me Jesus

Words and Music by
RICH MULLINS

times my life ___ just don't ___ make sense ___ at all, ___

Original key: G♯ minor. This edition has been transposed up one half-step to be more playable.

You have been ___ King of ___ my glo - ry. Won't You be ___

___ my Prince ___ of Peace? ___

8vb throughout

Some -

32

I'll Carry You

Words and Music by REBECCA ST. JAMES
and TEDD TJORNHOM

Moderately fast

I know that look ___ in your eyes.

I see the pain ___ be-hind ___ your smile. ___ Please ___

Come Quickly Lord

Words and Music by REBECCA ST. JAMES
and DAVID SMALLBONE

* Vocal line written one octave higher than sung

Peace

Words and Music by REBECCA ST. JAMES
and TEDD TJORNHOM

A - lone in — the val - ley, I cry for You — to fill
When the fires — rage, — when the storms sur - round — me, still

— me with Your peace.
— I live in peace.

So when the light - ning strikes,
Though the moun - tains fall,

54

Mirror

Words and Music by REBECCA ST. JAMES
and TEDD TJORNHOM

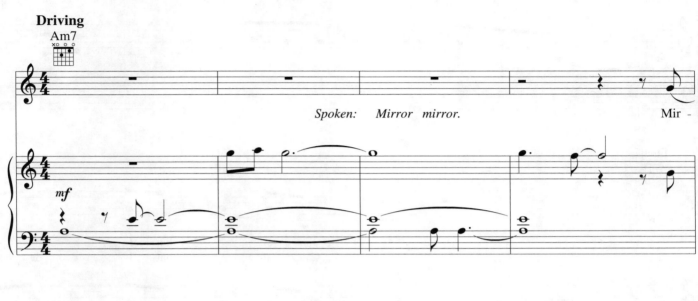

62

66

Lord You're Beautiful

Words and Music by
KEITH GREEN

Love to Love You

Words and Music by REBECCA ST. JAMES,
MICHAEL QUINIAN and TEDD TJORNHOM

Original key: G♭ major. This edition has been transposed up one half-step to be more playable.

Omega

Words and Music by REBECCA ST. JAMES
and TEDD TJORNHOM

Original key: F#major. This edition has been transposed down one half-step to be more playable.

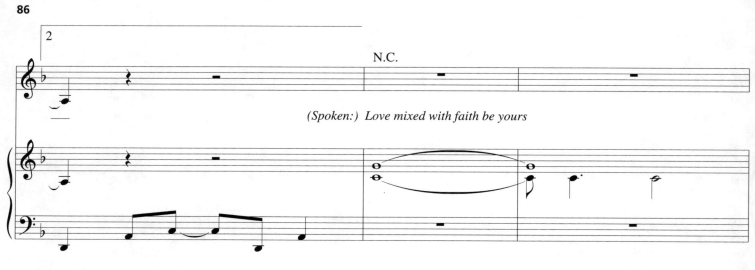

(Spoken:) Love mixed with faith be yours

From God   the Father   And

D.S. al Coda

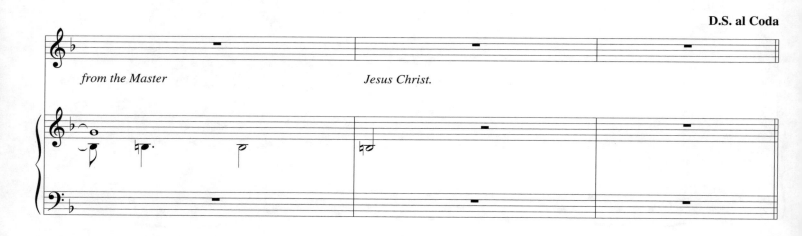

from the Master   Jesus Christ.

CODA E♭maj7

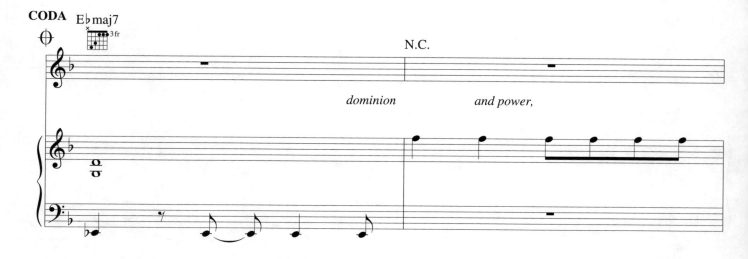

dominion   and power,